MEET THE AUTHORS

Both Patricia Barrett-Dragan (left) and Rosemary Dalton (right) are teachers, and make cooking a regular part of their classroom curriculum. They also teach Children's Cooking Classes in demonstration kitchens.

The recipes in this cookbook were tested with children and emphasize nutrition, meal and snack-planning, and how to read and follow simple directions. The authors worked closely with children to pick recipes "kids" like. Much of the artwork in the book was done by children in their classes.

Both authors live and work in the San Francisco Bay Area, and have written several other books for children.

THE PERFECT COOKBOOK FOR CHILDREN OF ALL AGES

- Basic cooking is covered in detail to get a young cook off to the right start.
- All kinds of recipes for breakfasts, lunches and dinners, plus desserts and snacks!
- Each chapter is illustrated with original drawings from a variety of young artists (see credits on page 183).
- For easy use this book lies flat when opened, contains one recipe per page and is printed in large easy-to-read type.
- Compact design—takes a minimum of counter space.

SATISFACTION GUARANTEE—If you are not completely satisfied with this book, your purchase price will gladly be refunded. Simply return it to us within 30 days along with your receipt.

To the loves in my life
Pete, Jan, Jim and Mom.

Rosemary

To my husband George,
my Dad and Mom, and all
my family. And to young
cooks everywhere: Have
fun with the adventure
of cooking!

Pat

The Kid's Cookbook

Yum! I Eat It.

Written by Patricia Barrett-Dragan and Rosemary Dalton
Spot illustrations by Patricia Barrett-Dragan
Full page art by Young Artists

© 1973
Revised 1982
Bristol Publishing Enterprises, Inc.

A Nitty Gritty® Cookbook
Published by
Bristol Publishing Enterprises, Inc.
P.O. Box 1737
San Leandro, California 94577

Printed in the United States of America.

ISBN 0-911954-68-6

Contents

Hi, Cooks and Cooks-to-be,

   We hope you'll like this cookbook, and will enjoy both the adventure of cooking and the fun of sharing what you make.

   The recipes are easy, and anyone can do them— as long as they can read and follow directions. If you are just learning to read, get someone to help you with the reading part. There are drawings to help you figure out cooking tools and directions.

   As soon as you read the next few pages, you are ready to start cooking. Have a great time!

1

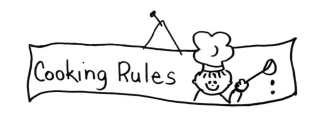

Cooking Rules

1. Whenever you get the urge to cook, check with your Mom or Dad. Someone else might want to use the kitchen.

2. Read the whole recipe before you start. If you don't understand something, get someone to help you.

3. If a recipe seems too hard for you to do alone, maybe your mother or brother or someone would help you. Get help especially for recipes using the electric beater or blender, unless you are cleared to use them alone.

Cooking Rules- Continued

4. Gather everything you need before you start. Then you won't have to look for something when your hands are sticky.

5. Keep a sponge handy in case you have to wipe something up in a hurry. Clean up when you are finished and put everything away.

6. Lots of people might have cooked the same recipe before you, but you can make it different by making your own special place mats, or decorations, or putting flowers on the table — or by adding

Cooking Rules-(Continued)

something that's just your own unique idea.

The following pages have drawings to explain cooking tools and cooking terms. Happy cooking!

Cooking Tools

 glass measuring cup for liquids

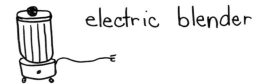 electric blender

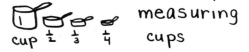 measuring cups
cup ½ ⅓ ¼

 electric frying pan

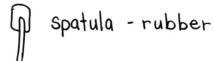 spatula - rubber

 frying pan or skillet

 spatula - metal or pancake turner

 pot or pan

 wooden spoon

Cooking Tools-(Continued)

cookie sheet
or pan

cooling rack

rolling pin

tongs

measuring spoons

timer

egg beater

grater

Cooking Tools - (Continued)

 soup ladle

 flour sifter

 mixing spoon

 egg separator

 electric mixer

 wire whip

 vegetable peelers

 apple corer

7

Cooking Tools- (Continued)

loaf pan

potato masher

cutting board

springalator pan

scoop

pot holder

double boiler

8

Cooking Terms

stir  to mix ingredients by moving a spoon around in a bowl.

beat  to stir foods fast with a spoon, or by using an egg beater or electric mixer

whip  to beat very fast using electric mixer or spoon

boil  to heat food in a pan or on top of the stove until large bubbles come to the top of the pan.

Cooking Terms - (Continued)

chop
dice
to cut food into little pieces

mince
to cut food into very small pieces

cube
to cut food into very little blocks or cubes

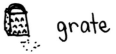 grate
to make food into tiny pieces by rubbing it up and down on a grater

11

Cooking Terms - (Continued)

toast   to brown food lightly

pare   to take the peeling off

sift   to put in a flour sifter and sift lumps
             out; sometimes to mix such ingredients
             as flour and salt.

Cooking Terms - (Continued)

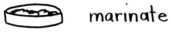 marinate   to soak food in a specific liquid often oil and vinegar

 cream   to mix until very smooth

 grease or butter a pan   to rub a little butter or margarine on the bottom of a pan to keep things from sticking (You can use a paper napkin to rub it on)

 pouring off grease   always ask an adult to help or to do this as grease splatters and can cause bad burns

Cooking Terms - (Continued)

simmer  to cook food on top of the stove on low heat until there are little bubbles around the edge of the pan

bake 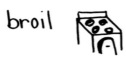 to cook in the oven

broil to cook food on the top rack of the oven in a broiler pan, with the door slightly open, and the oven knob on broil

Equivalents for Measuring

Note: Measurements for butter are marked on the
cube wrapper. 1 cup of butter = 2 cubes
$\frac{1}{2}$ cup of butter = 1 cube
$\frac{1}{4}$ cup of butter = $\frac{1}{2}$ cube

1 tablespoon = 3 teaspoons
4 tablespoons = $\frac{1}{4}$ cup
16 tablespoons = 1 cup

1 cup = $\frac{1}{2}$ pint (8 fluid ounces)
2 cups = 1 pint (16 fluid ounces)
2 pints = 1 quart
4 quarts = 1 gallon

15

Grapefruit and Honey

You need:

Grapefruit
Honey
Cherry

Put the grapefruit on a cutting board. Cut it in half. Spread 1 teaspoon of honey over each grapefruit half. Put a cherry on top.

17

Butter

Friends needed for muscle power.

You need:
½ pint whipping cream
Plastic container with lid
Dash of salt

Put the whipping cream into a plastic container with a good lid. Add a dash of salt. Close tightly. Shake. Keep shaking until you get yellow chunks of butter.

Pour off liquid. Mold into shape you want.

Spread on anything you like.

How to Crack Open an Egg

Hit it against the side of the bowl, tip up the shells and drop it in

or

Hold it over the bowl, hit it with the edge of a knife, and drop it in.

19

Eggs in a Nest

Put bread on cutting board. Cut a circle in the center of each slice with a cookie cutter.

Put 2 tablespoons of butter into frying pan on medium heat.

Fry bread slice on one side. Turn bread over. Add more butter if pan is too dry.

Turn heat to low. Break egg in the hole. Sprinkle with salt and pepper. Put cover on. Cook 3-5 minutes.

You need:

1 egg, 1 slice of bread per person

2 tablespoons butter

salt and pepper

big frying pan and cover

2 inch round cookie cutter

spatula

Hard Boiled Eggs

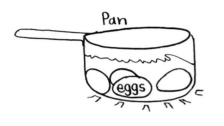

Pan

eggs

Put eggs in cold water, put pan on high heat until water boils. Then turn heat low and cook 15 minutes.* Drain eggs and run cold water over them. (This helps the shells to peel off without sticking.)

*For soft eggs only leave in water 2 or 3 minutes after you turned down heat.

21

Whirlpool Eggs

Fill a pan $\frac{2}{3}$ full of water. 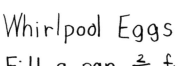 $\frac{2}{3}$ Boil. Break egg in a cup or small bowl. Stir water with a spoon to make a whirlpool.* Slip the egg into the water. Cover and turn heat to low. Put bread in the toaster. Cook egg about 3 minutes. Test the yolk with a fork. When egg is done as you like it, remove it with a slotted spoon. Put on buttered toast. Salt and pepper.

You need:
Egg
Toast
Slotted Spoon

*The whirlpool holds the egg together.

22

Scrambled Eggs

You need:
(To serve 4)
5 eggs
½ teaspoon salt
4 tablespoons butter
Frying pan

Melt 4 tablespoons of butter. Cool. Break the 5 eggs in a bowl. Add the salt and 2 tablespoons of the cooled butter. Beat with a wire whip or egg beater just enough to blend. Heat the rest of the butter in a frying pan on medium heat. Pour in the eggs. Use a fork to stir and keep from sticking. Cook eggs until they are the way your family likes them, stirring all the time. Cook them a little longer if you like your eggs dry, not juicy. For variety you can add bacon bits, small pieces of cheese, cooked vegetables or left-over meat. Cottage cheese is good too! Experiment!

23

French Toast

You need:

2 eggs
Dash of salt
½ cup milk
2 tablespoons
 butter
6 slices
 bread
frying pan

French Toast-(continued)

Melt butter in a frying pan. Take off heat. Break eggs in a bowl and beat with a fork. Add milk, salt, and stir. Dip bread slices in mixture. Coat both sides of the bread. Shake off extra mixture over bowl. Put bread in frying pan. Brown on both sides.

Serve with butter, honey, syrup, jam, or cinnamon and sugar. Peanut butter is good too.

Variations: Use whole wheat, rye or raisin bread. Or substitute orange juice for the milk. You can also make a great sandwich! Just put a filling such as ham and cheese between bread slices. Dip in batter and brown.

← bread
← cheese
← ham
← bread

Cinnamon Toast

Toast the bread. Spread it with butter. Sprinkle on the sugar and the cinnamon. (Watch out, not too much cinnamon!)

Mix the cinnamon and sugar together first, if you like.

You need:
2 slices bread
1 tablespoon butter
1 tablespoon sugar
1 teaspoon cinnamon

Pancake Art

Use a pancake mix. Follow the directions on the package. Heat griddle slowly while mixing batter. A griddle will not need greasing. If you use a frying pan heat when batter is ready. Add a little butter to the pan.

Pour pancake batter onto griddle or into pan using a spoon. Pour into shapes or creatures you like. Turn pancakes with a spatula when they are puffed up and full of bubbles. Brown other side. Eat with butter and jam or syrup.

You need:
Package of
pancake mix
Large spoon
Bowl
Griddle or
frying pan
imagination

Easy Fruit Salad

Put the oranges and pineapple in a bowl. Sprinkle jello over it and stir. Add cottage cheese and carton of cool whip. Stir and mix together. Put in the refrigerator to chill.
Serves 6-8.

You need:

1 box orange jello
small carton cottage cheese
small carton cool whip
2 cans mandarin oranges
1 20 ounce can crushed pineapple
Drain oranges and pineapple 1 hour.

Fresh Fruit Salad
Fun to do - takes time

You need:

Melon baller
Fresh fruit :
Cantaloupe
Bananas - 4
Watermelon - ($\frac{1}{4}$th of one)
Can of pineapple
   chunks
Any other fruit
 you want to add
Orange juice - $\frac{1}{4}$ cup
 1 tablespoon sugar

Fresh Fruit Salad (continued)

Cut the cantaloupe in half and clean out the seeds. Using the melon baller try to scoop out as many melon balls as possible. Put in a bowl. Do the same with the watermelon. Add the whole can of pineapple chunks with the juice. Peel and slice 4 bananas and add. Add 1 tablespoon sugar and $\frac{1}{4}$ cup orange juice. Mix all together and serve. Tastes better if it is in the refrigerator for about $\frac{1}{2}$ hour before you eat it. Serves 4-6.

Cantaloupe Salad (continued)

You can peel the cantaloupe if you like. If not, cut the cantaloupe into slices. Clean out the center of each slice Place in a dish. Fill the center of each slice with cottage cheese, or any filling you like. Place a cherry on top and serve. Special: change this into a dessert, with a scoop of your ice cream! if you like, and fill favorite

Parrot Pineapple Salad Boat
Don't cut the leaves off!

*Adult help needed for cutting.

You need:

1 fresh pineapple
1 can mandarin oranges
$\frac{1}{4}$ cup mayonnaise
1 teaspoon brown sugar
sharp knife
adult

Take the pineapple and cut it in half, all the way up through the leaves.

Then cut in half again. Now you should have 4 pieces with leaves on. Cut out the core.

Slice between the pineapple and the outer covering, leaving fruit loose in shell.

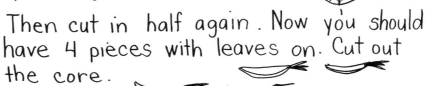

fruit cut loose

34

Parrot Salad - (Continued)

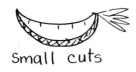

small cuts

Now slice small cuts down into the pineapple and put slices of orange in.

In a small bowl mix: the juice of the mandarin oranges, the mayonnaise, and the brown sugar. Mix until the lumps are gone.

Secret: If you have a wire whip, things blend quickly, with no lumps.

Pour sauce over pineapple boats and eat.
Real good.

Banana Split Salad

You need:
Banana
Cottage cheese
Small can of
fruit cocktail

Peel the banana. Slice it in half. Put it in a bowl. Put a scoop of cottage cheese on top. Pour the fruit cocktail over the banana and cottage cheese.

jingle

Jingle Bell Salad

Put the jello in a large bowl. Add 1 cup boiling water. Stir until jello dissolves. Add the strawberries. Stir until thawed out. Add the crushed pineapple. Dice the banana. Add it too. Pour <u>half</u> the mixture into a 8x8x2 inch pan. Put it in the refrigerator until jello sets.

You Need:

1 3 ounce package strawberry jello
1 half pint of sour cream
1 10-ounce package frozen strawberries
1 6-ounce can crushed pineapple
1 banana

Spread the sour cream over the top of the jello. Add the rest of the jello. Put in refrigerator until firm. Cut in squares and serve.

Astronaut Salad

You need:

Box of jello
1 cup boiling water
¾ cup cold water
empty orange juice cans for rocket molds
(or a popsicle mold)

Put jello in a bowl. Add 1 cup boiling water. Stir well. Add ¾ cup cold water. Stir. Pour this mixture into an empty orange juice can (so it looks like a rocket). Put in refrigerator to set. To unmold, dip into hot water quickly, then turn upside down on plate. Count down and eat.

carrot nosecone
lettuce launching
pad

Carrot Curls

You need:
Carrots-Washed
Peeler
Lemon juice
Sugar

Slice carrots or peel them very thin. Peel carrot the long way. Marinate* in lemon juice (or orange juice) and 1 teaspoon sugar. Serve chilled.

* Marinate means soak

Green Bean Salad

Open the 3 cans of beans. Drain liquid into sink. Put all the beans in a bowl. Add oil, vinegar, sugar, garlic powder, sliced onion and parsley. Mix. Let salad marinate for at least 2 hours. You don't have to refrigerate it. Serves 8-10 people.

You need:
1 8ounce can cut stringbeans
1 8 ounce can kidney beans
1 8 ounce can garbanzos
parsley-washed, dried, chopped
dash of garlic powder

$\frac{1}{2}$ cup olive oil
$\frac{1}{4}$ cup wine vinegar
2 teaspoons sugar
1 sliced onion

Crab or Shrimp Cocktail

Use a special glass or dish.

Fill glass or dish with crab or shrimp or both until glass is $\frac{3}{4}$ filled. Add the cocktail sauce until it just covers the seafood. Place the glass on a small dish with a lemon wedge.

You need:
shrimp or crab
lemon- cut in wedges
cocktail sauce

42

Tossed Salad

Wash the lettuce. Dry it. Tear it in small pieces and put them in a bowl. Add the tomato and other vegetables, and salt and pepper. Chill in refrigerator.

Pour salad dressing (1 tablespoon per person) over salad. Toss* with salad fork and spoon.

* Toss is when you lift salad a few inches with salad fork and spoon and then let it go. Repeat until well mixed.

You need:

1 or 2 kinds of lettuce
tomato - sliced
chopped celery or sliced radishes or other vegetables

Dressing you like

43

Mrs. Santa Claus's Nut Bread

You need:
- ½ cup sugar
- 1¼ cups milk
- 1½ cups chopped walnuts (You can buy them in packages all chopped)
- loaf pan
- 1 egg
- 3 cups bisquick

Preheat oven to 350°

In a big bowl mix the sugar, milk, bisquick and egg. Beat hard for 30 seconds. Stir in the walnuts. Butter the bottom of a loaf pan. Pour batter into pan. Bake 45-50 minutes, (until a toothpick stuck in the center of the bread comes out without crumbs on it).

Pumpkin Bread
Preheat oven to 350°.

You need:

2 cups pumpkin
1 cup salad oil
4 eggs
$\frac{2}{3}$ cup water
3 cups sugar
$3\frac{1}{2}$ cups sifted flour
2 teaspoons baking soda
$1\frac{1}{2}$ teaspoons salt
3 teaspoons nutmeg
3 teaspoons cinnamon
2 loaf pans 5×9

In a big bowl mix the pumpkin, oil, eggs, water and sugar.

Sift the rest of the ingredients together over wax paper. Add these slowly to the pumpkin mixture. Mix well. Pour into the 2 loaf pans. Bake at 350° for 1 hour.

46

Popovers

Great with dinner or for a snack.

Grease muffin pan and put in refrigerator to get cold.

Mix in a bowl

3 eggs OOO
1 cup milk
1 cup flour
½ teaspoon salt

This will be lumpy. Fill muffin pan cups ½ full.
Put in cold oven. Turn dial to 450.° Bake 30 minutes.
Don't peek!
Eat now! Eat with butter, jam, or honey.

47

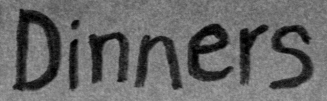

Dinners

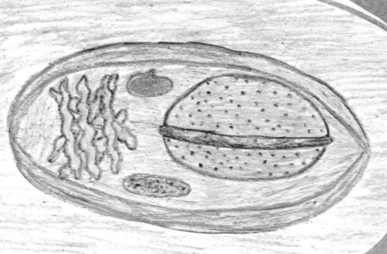

Hot Dogs

Boil enough water to cover hot dogs. Put hot dogs in the pan. Cover pan and turn off heat. Let stand 5 minutes. Serve.

You need:
hot dogs

hot dog buns

mustard, relish, whatever you like on hot dogs

Hot Dog Ka-bobs

Adult help may be needed to barbecue.

You need:
Pineapple chunks-canned
Canned potatoes
Cherry tomatoes
Teriyaki sauce
Skewers
Flat pan
Barbecue (or oven broiler)

Cut each hot dog into 4 parts. Put the skewer through the center of the hot dog. Push to end of skewer. Then put on pineapple chunk, potato, tomato. Continue until skewer is full.

Pour a little teriyaki sauce into a wide bowl. Dip each skewer in teriyaki sauce. Barbecue or broil.

50

Hot Dog Stew

You need:
6 hot dogs
1 onion, chopped
3 potatoes
3 tablespoons oil
1 8-ounce can
tomato sauce
2 cans vegetable
soup, undiluted
1½ soup cans
water
2 teaspoons
Worcestershire
sauce
1 teaspoon salt
⅛ teaspoon pepper

Cut hot dogs in ½ inch slices. Peel and chop onion. Peel and dice potatoes. Keep potatoes in cool water.

Heat oil in large saucepan. Add onions and cook till clear.

Add tomato sauce, soup, water, potatoes, Worcestershire sauce, salt and pepper. Cook 20 minutes on medium heat with pan covered.

Add hot dogs. Turn heat to simmer. Cook slowly another 15 minutes.

Pigs in Blankets

You need:
Hot dogs
Bisquick or other biscuit mix

Pigs in Blankets - (Continued)

Boil enough hot water to cover hot dogs. Turn off. Put hot dogs in pan and cover. Let stand 5 minutes. Drain water off.

Mix biscuit dough according to package directions. Put dough on wax paper. Put another piece on top. Pat dough to $\frac{1}{4}$ inch thick. Remove top paper. Cut dough into 3x4 inch strips. Roll a piece around each hot dog. Let the tip of the hot dog show at each end. Pinch the end of the dough to seal it. Put on cookie sheet, sealed edge down. Bake 15 minutes at 450°. Eat with mustard and relish.

Chicken Wings Teriyaki

You need:

2 pounds chicken wings, or 14 wings

¼ cup salad oil

¼ cup

1 cup teriyaki sauce (use ½ cup first, ½ cup later.)

Wash and dry wings. Place in large baking pan. Add the salad oil and ½ cup teriyaki sauce. Place in oven and bake 45 minutes at 350°. ✸ Stir wings and add another ½ cup of teriyaki sauce after 25 minutes. These are delicious!

54

Teriyaki Beef Strips

You need:

sirloin steak

wooden skewers

1 bottle teriyaki sauce (small)

barbecue or hibachi

adult help needed for cooking

You can prepare the meat ahead of time. Cut the steak into small rectangles ▭ about 1 by 2 inches. Thread about 3 pieces onto a skewer. Place in a flat dish. Cover and refrigerate. About an hour before you are ready to barbecue, place the skewers in a shallow pan. Pour the teriyaki sauce over the meat. Leave skewers in sauce until you barbecue.

Cook on one side, then the other. They cook quickly and are real good – so have plenty of skewers ready !!

55

Baked Pork Chops

You need:
6 pork chops
1 teaspoon salt
$\frac{1}{2}$ teaspoon pepper
1 can cream of mushroom soup
ovenproof casserole or baking pan

Sprinkle salt and pepper on the chops. Brown chops in the oven for $\frac{1}{2}$ hour at 350°. Turn the chops over after 15 minutes. Spread the can of soup over the chops and add $\frac{1}{2}$ soup can of water. Cover and bake for 1 hour at 350°. Serves 4-6.

Variation: Use cream of celery or cream of potato soup instead of cream of mushroom soup, if you like.

56

turtle soup

Barbecued Pork Kabobs

Variations: This recipe can also be made with beef or chicken cubes instead of pork.

You need:
skewers
2 pounds pork, cut in 1 inch cubes
1 small onion, sliced
2 ½ tablespoons brown sugar
2 tablespoons soy sauce
2 cloves garlic
Large bowl and cover
Adult help to barbecue

Barbecued Pork Kabobs (continued)

Mix together in a large bowl: sliced onion, brown sugar, soy sauce. Chop the garlic. Put meat into the mixture. Make sure meat is well coated with mixture. Cover. Leave in refrigerator about $\frac{1}{2}$ day.

About 2 hours before dinner, put meat on skewers. Leave small spaces in between. Have an adult start the barbecue. When the coals are hot place skewers on the grate. Barbecue 15 minutes. Keep turning the skewers so they brown on all sides. Serves 4.

Hamburger

You need:
1 pound hamburger
1 teaspoon salt
$\frac{1}{4}$ teaspoon pepper
4 hamburger buns, toasted *

Divide hamburger into 4 parts. Shape into hamburger patties.

Cook in a frying pan on medium heat or in an oven broiled. (Also good barbecued). When one side is done (brown) turn and cook other side until brown. Salt and

Hamburger (continued)

pepper hamburgers. Serve with mustard, catsup, pickle relish, or whatever you like.

* To toast hamburger buns put them on a cookie sheet and put under broiler until golden brown. Remember to use pot holders!!

Variations: Some good additions to hamburgers are: cheese, chili, beans, pickles, tortilla chips, pineapple, lettuce, tomato.

Spaghetti for 6

Sauce takes a while.

Super chef recipe!

You need:

$\frac{1}{4}$ cup chopped onion
$\frac{1}{4}$ cup salad or olive oil
1 pound ground beef
clove of garlic-chopped
4-ounce can of mushrooms
2 cups canned tomatoes
1 8-ounce can tomato sauce
1 6-ounce can tomato paste

1 teaspoon salt
$\frac{1}{4}$ teaspoon oregano
$\frac{1}{4}$ teaspoon pepper
$\frac{1}{8}$ teaspoon basil
$\frac{1}{8}$ teaspoon thyme
1 pound package spaghetti
grated cheese

62

Spaghetti - (Continued)

Chop ¼ cup of onions. Put ¼ cup of oil into large frying pan. Slowly fry on low heat until onions look clear. Add the ground beef, garlic chopped fine, cans of mushrooms, tomatoes, tomato sauce, tomato paste, salt, oregano, pepper, basil, and thyme.

Cook these ingredients on <u>low</u> heat for 2 hours. Stir once in a while. Cook spaghetti, using directions on package. Drain spaghetti in colander. Mix spaghetti and sauce. Serve with grated parmesan cheese.

Sloppy Joes

Heat oil in frying pan, on medium heat. Add onion. Cook until clear. Add hamburger. Stir meat. Cook, stirring often, until brown.

Add catsup and tomato sauce. Stir mixture. Cook until hot and bubbly.

Spoon over hamburger buns.

If you like your buns toasted, put in oven a few minutes before mixture is done (when you add tomato sauce to hamburger). Watch buns carefully! Serves 4.

You need:
1½ pounds hamburger
1 tablespoon oil
2 - 8 ounce cans tomato sauce
2 tablespoons catsup
1 chopped onion
8 toasted bun halves (4 whole buns)

64

Easy Fish

Preheat oven to 450°. Thaw the fish if frozen. Rinse fish in cold water and pat it dry with paper towels.

Whip the egg and oil together in a shallow bowl with a fork. Put the flour* in another shallow bowl. Dip the pieces of fish in flour, then in egg mixture, then in flour again. Put the coated fish on a cookie sheet. (Non-stick is best). Bake for 6 minutes. Turn fish with a spatula. Sprinkle with salt and pepper. Bake 3-4 minutes more. Serves 4.

You need:
1 pound fish fillets, such as flounder, sole.
1 egg
3 tablespoons cooking oil
½ cup flour* (or cornmeal, pancake mix, cracker crumbs)
Salt and pepper
Cookie sheet

Macaroni and Cheese
Preheat oven to 350°

You need:
1½ cups elbow macaroni

colander

¾ cup milk

grater

1½ cup grated sharp cheddar cheese

3 tablespoons butter

*salt and pepper, too, if you like

Cook 1½ cups of elbow macaroni according to directions on package. Drain macaroni in colander.

Put wax paper under grater. Grate cheddar cheese until you have 1½ cups.

Mix together in a casserole dish: milk, noodles, grated cheese, and butter.*Bake at 350° for 35 minutes. Serves 6.

67

Tacos

If you have a lazy susan put your taco fillings on it. Put it in the center of the table. Everyone can spin it to get to their favorite fillings.

You need:

Taco shells already packaged and shaped

1 pound ground chuck

grated cheese

olives-chopped

tomatoes

shredded lettuce

hot sauce ?

Taco sauce for some!

Turn frying pan on medium heat. Put in hamburger in small bits. Brown it, stirring often. Salt and pepper. Drain off fat. Put hamburger in a bowl.

Heat the taco shells according to the directions on the package.

Grate cheddar cheese.

Open can of chopped olives.

Cut tomatoes in wedges. Peel and chop onion.

Put things in small bowls. Everyone puts their favorite things on own taco.

69

Broiled Lamb Chops

You need:
lamb chops,
1 or 2 per
person

Take the broiler pan and rack out of the oven. Preheat the oven 10 minutes on broil. Put the chops on the broiler rack. Put the rack in the oven on the top rack slot (closest to heat). Broil the chops with the oven door partly open. Cook half the time on one side, half on the other. Sprinkle with salt and pepper. Broil chops 1 inch thick 12-15 minutes. Broil chops 1½-2 inches thick 20-35 minutes. Serve with tomato slices or mint jelly.

70

Lamb Chop Meal

for 4-6   Preheat oven to 425.°

You need:
- 4 carrots – peeled and quartered
- 1 onion – peeled and quartered
- 4 potatoes – peeled and halved
- 4-6 lamb chops
- oven proof casserole

Put flour*on wax paper. Dip lamb chops in flour on both sides. Put lamb chops into casserole dish. Bake 15 minutes. Take casserole out (use a potholder!) and put on top of stove. Have someone help you pour the grease into an empty can or milk carton. Put potatoes, carrots, and onion on bottom of pan. Put lamb chops on top. Add 2 tablespoons water. Cover. Bake at 350° for 1½ hours. Take cover off for last 15 minutes.

* salt and pepper, too, if you like

71

Easy Green Beans

Cut ends off beans. Cut in half.
Wash beans. In a pan heat about
2 inches of water and ½
teaspoon salt. Boil water.
Add beans and bring to
a boil. Cover and
cook 20 minutes
or until tender.
Drain liquid, add
butter, and serve.

I eat
it yum

73

Glazed Carrots

Cut the tops off the carrots and scrub or peel. Cut into slices, halves, or rectangles. Cook in a heavy covered pan with enough water to cover them. If whole, cook 15-20 minutes. If sliced, cook 8-10 minutes. Drain if necessary.

In a small pot melt butter and add the brown sugar. Heat 3 minutes, and add to carrots. Mix and serve.

74

Corn on the Cob

You need:

Ears of corn, husked

Boiling water

Boil enough water to cover the corn. Remove the husks and threads from the corn. Put the corn in the water. When water boils again cook 5 minutes longer. You know corn is done when you stick a fork in the kernels and they're tender.

Drain the corn. Serve with lots of butter.

St. Patrick's Day Surprises
Preheat oven to 425°

You need:
Baking potatoes
Butter or
Sour cream

Wash potatoes and scrub skin. Dry. Cut a little slice off each end to let steam escape. Bake 40 minutes to 1 hour at 425.°

You know a baked potato is done when you stick a fork in and it is not hard.

Serve with lots of butter or sour cream ~ with a
GREEN NAPKIN or
DECORATED PLACEMAT.

76

Yams and Pineapple

You need:
1 big can yams
1 small can
crushed
pineapple
marshmallows
oven
casserole

Open and drain the can of yams. Put yams in casserole. Open can of crushed pineapple and add to the yams. With a potato masher, mash the yams and pineapple together. Do only a few times. If you have large marshmallows, place 12 on top of the yams. Put into the oven uncovered. Bake at 350° for 25 minutes. Check the casserole after 20 minutes. If very brown, remove from oven.

Mashed Potatoes

You need:
6 potatoes
Potato masher
4 tablespoons
 butter
$\frac{1}{3}$ cup milk
salt and
 pepper

Mashed Potatoes (continued)

Wash and peel 6 potatoes. Cut them in half and place in a 2 quart pot ½ filled with water. Add 1 teaspoon salt. Boil the potatoes about 20-25 minutes. Check at 20 minutes. Use a fork and carefully pierce the potato for softness. They should be soft and not too mushy. When done, drain the water. Add the butter, milk, and a shake of pepper. Mash with potato masher until they are fluffy. Taste, and add more salt if needed. Pile lightly and high into a serving dish. Place 2 tablespoons of butter on top of potatoes and serve.

Open Faced Sandwiches

Fun to serve for something special

Cut crusts off slices of bread. Spread slice with butter, mayonnaise or mustard. Put on a slice of ham, cheese, salami, or your favorite spread. Cut the sandwich on a diagonal. Put on a plate. Decorate with parsley, olives, lettuce, anything you want.

You need:
Bread
mayonnaise
butter
mustard
ham, cheese,
whatever you
like

Dragon-Toasted Cheese
(Grilled Cheese)

Heat the frying pan on low, with a teaspoon of butter, until it just melts. Butter 2 slices of bread on 1 side only. Put 1 slice in the pan and put the sliced cheese on top. Place the other slice of bread on top with the buttered side up. Slowly brown the sandwich on one side, and then turn it to the other side. Use a spatula. As soon as the sandwich is brown, take it out of the pan and place it on a dish. Serve with a pickle. Good with potato chips too.

You need:
Cheese
Butter
Bread

Peanut Butter

Shell the peanuts. Put the peanuts in a blender. Add the oil. Turn on blender. Blend until chunky or smooth. Taste. Add salt if necessary.

You need:

1 adult + 1 blender

2 cups shelled fresh roasted peanuts

or

2 cups packaged salted peanuts

2 tablespoons salad oil

Use walnuts, pecans, etc. to make other nut butters.

Fluff 'n Nutter Sandwich
(Peanut Butter and Marshmallow Cream)

Be careful! Very sticky!

You need:

2 slices bread
peanut butter
Marshmallow
cream (comes
in a jar)

Spread peanut butter on one slice of bread. Spread marshmallow cream on the other slice. Put slices together and eat.

Peanut Butter and Banana Sandwich

You need:

2 slices
bread.

peanut
butter,

banana

Spread peanut butter on bread. Peel and slice a banana. Put the slices on top of the peanut butter. Put a second piece of bread on top. Cut in half and eat.

Zoo Sandwiches
Fun to do for birthday parties, picnics

You need:
Filling you
like: tuna,

peanut
butter and
jam, etc.

3 slices bread
for each
sandwich

animal or shape
cookie cutters or
knife

Cut out animal shapes or shapes you like. Cut 3 shapes the same for each sandwich. Use cookie cutters or knife.

Spread filling on 1 sandwich slice. Put another slice on top. Spread on more filling. Put third slice on.

Now sandwich will stand up on plate.

Picnic Sandwich
Greatest ever!

Serves 6

You need:
1 long loaf of sour French bread
About 1½ pounds of mixed lunch meats sliced paper thin
mustard
mayonnaise

Slice the loaf of bread down the middle, but <u>not</u> all the way through. Gently open the bread so that it is flat but not separated. Spread with mustard and mayonnaise on both sides. Be generous. Lay on the layers of lunch-meat. Spread the layers with a small amount of mayonnaise. Continue until all the layers are on. Close the loaf and slice in 2 inch wedges, but not all the way through. Everyone can pull off his own sandwich. Boy, is this good!

Hot Dog Spread

You need:

5 hot dogs

blender + adult (unless you are cleared to use it alone)

$\frac{1}{2}$ cup mayonnaise

1 tablespoon mustard

$\frac{1}{2}$ cup sweet pickle relish

Fill a pan with enough water to cover hot dogs. Boil water. Put hot dogs in and cover pan. Turn off heat. Let stand 5 minutes. Slice hot dogs into small pieces. Put hot dogs and all other ingredients in blender. Blend until smooth. Serve on crackers.

Meatballs
Make this at the table.

You need:

- 1 pound of hamburger
- $\frac{1}{4}$ cup milk
- $\frac{1}{2}$ cup bread crumbs
- $\frac{1}{4}$ cup Parmesan cheese
- 1 teaspoon salt
- toothpicks
- catsup and mustard
- 1 electric frying pan - on table

In a bowl mix hamburger, milk, salt, egg, breadcrumbs and cheese. Roll into meatballs.

Put 2 tablespoons of oil in pan. Turn temperature of pan to 325° Put meatballs in.

Cook slowly. Turn until light brown on all sides. (About 15 minutes.)

Take out with a spatula. Put on plate. Serve with toothpicks. Dip into catsup or mustard.

Little Pizzas

You need:

- 1 package English muffins
- 1 8 ounce can pizza topping or
- 1 8 ounce can of marinara sauce
- Grated or sliced cheese
- Whatever else you like.

Open muffins. On each half spread 2-3 tablespoons of sauce. Sprinkle grated or sliced mozzarella cheese on top. For cheese pizzas, broil now.

Otherwise, add salami, sliced olives, sausage, or anything else you like.

Broil until bubbly. Watch carefully.

91

Little Bologna Rolls

Spread the cheese on the slices of bologna. <u>Secret</u>: Don't use too much. About 1 tablespoon is enough. Roll the bologna by taking 1 end and starting to roll it up, slowly and tightly. After it is rolled up, cut it into 1 inch slices. Put the small slices on a dish. Makes a good snack.

Artichoke Leaf Nibbles

You need:
1 cooked
artichoke
4 flat dishes
1 small dish
1 for center dip

Wash artichoke. Trim top stem leaving $\frac{1}{2}$ inch. Boil in 6 inches of water for 45 minutes with cover on pan. Drain and cool. Carefully peel off leaves one at a time. Place the leaves around the dish. Put your favorite dip in the center. Dip one leaf at a time into dip. Good finger food.

Cheese Puffs

You need:
1 5 ounce jar
Old English
Cheese Spread
$\frac{1}{2}$ cube butter or
margarine
$\frac{1}{2}$ teaspoon salt
$\frac{1}{2}$ cup flour
electric mixer
(if you are
cleared to use it)
Cookie sheet

Mix butter and cheese until smooth and creamy. Add the rest of the ingredients and mix until smooth. (An electric mixer makes this easier).

Roll mixture into little balls. Place on cookie sheet and put in refrigerator for 2 hours. Take from refrigerator when ready to eat. Bake in a 400° oven for 10 minutes. These are good snacks.

Ham and Cheese Snacks

Take one slice of ham and one slice of cheese. Add one more slice of ham, then cheese. Make this about 6 layers high. Now cut into little squares. Put a toothpick in each square. So good you want to eat and eat and eat....

You need:

sliced ham
sliced cheese

Stuffed Celery

You need:
celery
peanut
butter or
cheese
spread

Clean the celery by washing it carefully, one piece at a time. Dry the stalks. Cut off the leaf part and trim the bottom.

Now you have a clean stalk of celery ready to fill. Use cheese spread or peanut butter. Fill the stalks. Put them on a dish. They are ready to eat.

Stuffed Eggs

Bet you'll make more —

You need:

2 eggs

⅛ teaspoon salt

¼ cup mayonnaise

lettuce leaf

paprika

Hard boil the eggs. Peel and cut eggs in half. ☺ Take out the yellow centers carefully. Put them in a bowl and mash with a fork until smooth. Add the salt and mayonnaise and mix well— no lumps. Fill the 4 halves with filling. Pile it high and easy with a teaspoon. Place on a clean lettuce leaf. Sprinkle with paprika.

98

Roll'em Up Bread Swirls

You need:
bread
tuna or
deviled
egg spread
knife
rolling pin

Take a slice of bread. Cut off all the crusts. Save the crusts in a plastic bag. They can be used for bread crumbs. Roll over the bread one or twice until it is flattened. Put 1 tablespoon of tuna or deviled egg mix on the bread. Spread thin and not quite to the edge. Add more spread if needed. Roll the bread from the bottom up. Cut slices off the roll. Put on a dish and decorate with lettuce or parsley.

99

Clam Dip

Chop 1 teaspoon of onion very fine. Set aside. Open the can of clams. Drain the clam juice into a small bowl. Save 2 tablespoons of the juice and mix in clams, cream cheese, onion, Worcestershire sauce. A beater or blender makes the dip smoother.

You need:
10½ ounce can minced clams
8 ounce package cream cheese
1 teaspoon finely chopped onion
1 teaspoon Worcestershire sauce
beater or blender

101

Guacomole
This is a favorite dip!

You need:

3 medium ripe avocados
1 medium-sized tomato
1 small onion – chopped fine
2 tablespoons lemon juice
½ teaspoon salt
Dash of red hot sauce (Mexican hot sauce)

Peel and cube avocados. Save the seeds. Cube the tomato also. Put together in a bowl. Add finely chopped onion, lemon juice, salt, and the dash or 2 of hot sauce. Mix and serve with taco chips for dipping.

Guacomole - (Continued)

Extra added special:

Take the seeds that you saved and cleaned. Put 3 toothpicks in the seed just above the middle. Put the flat side down. Place the seed in a glass. Fill it almost to the top with water. Keep the glass filled with water every day. Watch the seed root and grow into a beautiful plant.

Deviled Ham Dip

Mix all ingredients together until smooth. Put in a clean bowl. Serve with your favorite crackers or fresh vegetables.

You need:

1 4½ ounce can deviled ham	1 tablespoon catsup
1 3 ounce package cream cheese	1 teaspoon Worcestershire sauce

Tuna Dip

You need:
1 7 ounce can tuna
$\frac{1}{2}$ cup mayonnaise
1 teaspoon Worcestershire sauce
$\frac{1}{4}$ teaspoon salt

Open tuna and drain the oil. Put tuna into bowl, and add mayonnaise, Worcestershire sauce and salt. Mix together and use as a dip.

Strawberry Dip

Wash strawberries in a colander. Leave stems on. Dry.

Put strawberries in a dish. Put sour cream in a small dish. And put brown sugar in a small dish.

To eat, pick up a strawberry by the stem. Dip first in sour cream and then in brown sugar.

Keep going . . .

You need:
Bowl of strawberries
1 pint sour cream
Brown sugar
Colander

Orange - Banana Dunk

Put the toppings and garnishes into paper cups. Peel the banana or orange and dunk away!

You need:

small paper cups
banana and or orange
toppings: chocolate, whipped cream, jam, whatever you like.
garnishes: coconut, nuts, jello powder, use your imagination!

Chocolate Chip Cookies
Preheat oven to 375.°

You need:

2 cups sifted flour
1 teaspoon soda
$\frac{1}{2}$ teaspoon salt
1$\frac{1}{2}$ cubes butter
1 cup brown sugar-packed
$\frac{1}{4}$ cup white sugar
1 egg
1$\frac{1}{2}$ teaspoon vanilla
1 6 ounce package semi-sweet chocolate chips
$\frac{1}{2}$ cup nuts-chopped

In a bowl mix the butter until creamy. Slowly add the sugars. Keep mixing until light and fluffy. Add the egg and vanilla. Mix well. Sift all the dry things and slowly add them. Stir in chocolate chips and nuts. Drop from a teaspoon on a greased cookie sheet. Bake at 375° for 10-12 minutes, (until golden brown).

The Cookie Special

Wheelies

Preheat oven to 375°.

A good snack to take with you wherever you go.

You need:

1 package fudge brownie mix

1 package walnut or pecan halves (about 30 nuts) 40 if you use family size mix.

Mix brownie mix according to directions on package, but leave out the chopped nuts. Drop rounded teaspoonfuls of dough on a cookie sheet. Put a walnut or pecan half on top of each cookie. Bake at 375° for 10-12 minutes.

Gingerbread Cookies

Preheat oven to 375°

You need:
1 cup shortening
1 cup brown sugar
3 eggs
2 cups molasses
8 cups flour
2 teaspoons soda
1 teaspoon salt
2 teaspoons ginger
2 tablespoons cinnamon

In a bowl, cream sugar and shortening. Add eggs and molasses. Mix. Sift dry ingredients over wax paper. Add to mixture and stir well. Put in refrigerator until cold.

Roll out on cutting board to ½ inch thick. Cut out with gingerbread boy cookie cutter. Stick raisins on for eyes, buttons. Bake at 375° 8-10 minutes.

111

Oatmeal Cookies

Preheat oven to 350°.

You need:

- ¾ cup shortening
- 1 cup brown sugar
- ½ cup white sugar
- 1 egg
- ¼ cup water
- 1 teaspoon vanilla
- 1 cup flour
- 1 teaspoon salt
- ½ teaspoon baking soda
- 3 cups rolled oats

Mix ingredients in a bowl in the order listed. Drop by teaspoonfuls on a greased cookie sheet. Bake in 350° oven for 12-15 minutes.

Cookies 5¢

112

Peanut Butter Cookies

Preheat oven to 375°

Mix together:
¼ cup shortening
¼ cup peanut butter
¼ cup brown sugar
1 egg, beaten

Add to it:
$\frac{3}{4}$ cup sifted flour
¼ teaspoon baking powder
$\frac{1}{8}$ teaspoon soda
$\frac{1}{8}$ teaspoon salt.

Chill in refrigerator about 1 hour. Take out Roll into balls. Place 3 inches apart on a cookie sheet. Press with a fork. Bake at 375° for 10 – 12 minutes.

113

Sugar Cookies
Preheat oven to 400°

1. <u>Mix well with mixer:</u>
   3/4 cup soft shortening
   1 cup sugar
   2 eggs
   1/2 teaspoon vanilla or
      lemon flavoring

2. <u>Sift together and stir in:</u>
   2 1/4 cups sifted flour
   1 teaspoon baking
      powder
   1 teaspoon salt

3. Chill for 1 hour. Place on ungreased baking sheet. Sprinkle with sugar. Bake at 400° for 6-8 minutes. Makes 4-6 dozen.

Little Moon Cookies

Preheat oven to 325°.

You need:
- 2 cubes butter
- wooden spoon
- 1 cup powdered sugar
- $\frac{1}{2}$ teaspoon salt
- 1c nuts — (your favorite)
- 1 tablespoon vanilla
- 2 cups flour
- Ungreased cookie pan

In a bowl mix butter until soft, using wooden spoon. Slowly add powdered sugar and salt. Mix well. Add nuts and 1 tablespoon vanilla.

Then add 2 cups of flour. Mix well. If you want clean hands make good mixers.

With your hands shape into crescents)) (little moons) or balls. Place on <u>ungreased</u> cookie sheet, or pan.

Bake at 325° for 15-18 minutes. <u>Don't brown</u>! Roll into powdered sugar.

115

Strawberry Shortcake

You need:
1 basket of
strawberries
sugar
shortcake
dessert cups
(in bakery
section of
market)
shaker can
whipped cream

Wash and dry the berries. Pick the stems out. Put berries in a bowl and crush them with a fork. Add a little sugar. Taste to check if it is sweet enough.

Put dessert cups on plates. Spoon berries on, and then squirt with whipped cream. Put a few berries on top. Everyone loves it....

117

Fortune Cakes

Preheat oven to 350°

You need:
Flat bottomed
ice cream
cones
1 box of
cake mix
pencil or pen
white paper
cut in little
white strips
$\frac{1}{2}$ inch x
2 inches

"You will be very lucky."

"Hmm, work harder."

Mine says, "Take a trip."

Write your own fortunes on strips of paper.
Make recipe for 1 package cake mix.
Fill cones $\frac{1}{2}$ full. Put cones in cake pan.
Fold fortunes. Put 1 in each cone. Poke
down into batter.

118

Fortune Cakes - (Continued)

Bake in 350° oven for 1 hour or until lightly browned.

   Don't eat your fortune! You can wrap it in foil and leave it partly sticking out of the cupcake.

   Sample fortunes:

(Have fun thinking up your own).

You win a free trip to the Moon.

You may eat 1 more cupcake.

Recycle this fortune. It's not any good anyway.

Heart Cake

You need:
Cake mix*
frosting mix *

*flavors you like

Make the cake according to directions on package. Pour batter into one 8 inch round pan and one 8 inch square pan. Bake as directed on package. Then remove cake from oven and let it cool.

To make the cake into a heart shape put the square cake on a plate with the point toward you. ◇ Cut the round layer in half. Arrange like this ♡. Make the frosting. Frost and eat. You'll love it!

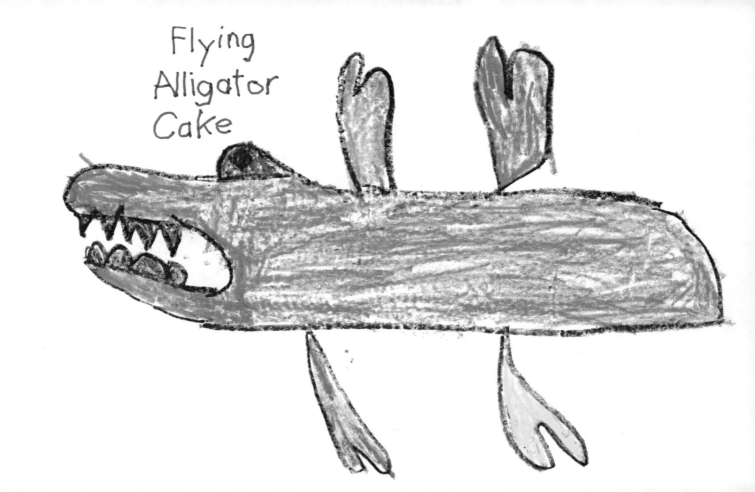

Flying
Alligator
Cake

Merry-Go-Round Cake

You need:

1 box of animal crackers

Decorating tubes filled with different colors of icing

Cake mix you like

Frosting mix

Colored straws

Merry-Go-Round Cake - (Continued)

Buy a box of animal crackers. Put them on a piece of wax paper. Decorate the crackers with the tubes of icing. Take your time. When they are done bake your favorite 2 layer cake. Put your favorite icing on it.

Put the animals on the cake, pushing lightly into the icing. If you want to decorate the top, use colored straws cut in half. Put a straw behind each animal.

Make a top out of colored paper. Use a dinner plate (trace around it) to make a circle. Slit the paper on one side. (◯ ← slit is cut). Slightly overlap the slit and fasten. ◔ Put the circus top on the cake and you have created a masterpiece!

123

Upside Down Cake

You need:

1 yellow cake mix
1 can pineapple rings
1 cube butter
1 cup brown sugar
skillet
1 package pecan halves

124

Preheat oven to 325°

Get a bowl. Make cake according to directions on package. Set aside.

In a skillet melt butter. Add brown sugar. Stir until mixed. Take pan off stove. Add nuts.

Drain juice from pineapple. Spread out pineapple in skillet on top of sugar, butter, and nuts.

Pour batter into skillet. Bake for ½ hour at 325.°

Right side up now.

Little Pudding Cakes

You need:

1 package cake mix - kind you like
1 package pudding mix. (Pick flavors that go together, like vanilla cake and lemon or chocolate pudding).
powdered sugar
muffin tin
cupcake papers

Make cupcakes according to directions on cake mix. Put cupcake papers in muffin tin. Pour batter in until each cupcake paper is half full. Bake as directed on package. Remove cupcakes and cool.

Cut a deep circle out of the top of each cupcake. 🧁. Make pudding mix. Pour into center of each cupcake. Put top back on. Sprinkle with powdered sugar and eat.

You need:

2 cups sugar
3 cups flour
1 teaspoon salt
2 teaspoons baking powder
2 teaspoons baking soda
2 teaspoons cinnamon
2 teaspoons nutmeg
1½ cups cooking oil
1 cup walnuts
4 eggs
2 cups grated carrots

Carrot Cake
Preheat oven to 350°

Peel carrots. Grate enough to make 2 cups. Set aside.

Sift into a bowl: sugar, flour, salt, baking powder, baking soda, cinnamon, and nutmeg. Add 2 eggs and half the oil. Stir. Add the rest of the eggs and oil. Stir again. Add nuts and grated carrots. Mix well. Pour into a greased 9x13 inch pan. Bake 1 hour at 350°.

127

Berries and Cream

Wash the berries in the colander. Drain. Put them in a bowl. Add milk or cream. Add sugar if needed.

You need:

berries *
colander
cream or
  milk
sugar

* Use any berries you like!

Other fruits are good this way too!

129

Applesauce

Take 6 apples. Peel and core.*
Slice the apples. Cook in water
until tender. Drain and mash with
a fork. Add the sugar and cinnamon.

You need:
6 apples
½ cup sugar
½ cup water
cinnamon-
just a
sprinkle.

* Core means to
take the seeds out.

Variation: Add orange juice instead of water
for a real taste treat!

Graham-Apples

You need:
3 graham crackers
small can applesauce
can of whipped cream

Spread applesauce on a graham cracker. Put a graham cracker on top. Put applesauce on this cracker too. Then put third graham cracker on top. Spray whole cracker-applesauce cookie with whipped cream. Spread with a knife. Keep in refrigerator 20 minutes, then eat.

131

Fruit Cobbler

Great even if you don't live in a shoe!
Preheat oven to 350°

You need:

1 cube butter, melted
1 cup flour
1 cup milk
2 teaspoons
  baking powder
sprinkle of salt
1 can of your
  favorite pie filling
oven proof casserole

Fruit Cobbler - (Continued)

Melt the butter in a pan over very low heat. Take it off the heat. Pour it in the bottom of the casserole. In a bowl mix the flour, milk, baking powder and salt. Pour this mixture over the butter. Pour the pie filling on top. Bake at 350° for 45 minutes.

Pumpkin Pie

In a bowl, combine pumpkin pie mix with eggs and evaporated milk as directed in the recipe on the can. Pour filling into pie crust, or set it aside while you prepare a pie crust using 2 pie sticks. Follow the directions for 1 pie shell, but <u>do</u> <u>not</u> prick crust. Pour pumpkin filling into crust. Bake as directed in recipe.

You need:
1 30-ounce can pumpkin pie mix
2 eggs
1 small can evaporated milk
1 9-inch unbaked pie <u>crust</u> <u>or</u> 1 package pie sticks

Chocolate Pie

You need:

1 5½ ounce package of chocolate pudding and pie filling
baked 9 inch pie shell
Can of spray on whipped cream.

Make pie filling according to the directions on the package. Cool 5 minutes. Pour into cool baked pie shell. Put in refrigerator for 3 hours. Cut and serve with whipped cream on top.

Or, make a whipped cream design on the pie.

Peanut Butter Cup

candy

Peanut Butter Balls

Mix and stir everything together. Roll into balls. If you like, put peanuts on top or a peanut inside the candy ball.

Variations: You can vary the taste by rolling the balls into coconut, granola, chocolate chips, banana chips, etc!

Coconut Fudge

You need:

1 medium-size potato

1 package powdered sugar

1 teaspoon vanilla

⅓ cup grated coconut

4 ounces of chocolate candy

Peel a potato. Cut it in half, and in half again. Cook it for 20-25 minutes in a pot about half full of water. Mash the potato in a bowl. Add the powdered sugar. Mix well (use your clean fingers). Add the vanilla and coconut.

Pat the candy into an 8 inch by 10 inch buttered pan. Melt the chocolate in a double boiler or in a pan sitting in a skillet with water in it. Pour chocolate over the candy. Cut into squares.

S'mores

You need:

8 graham crackers
2 small chocolate bars
4 hot toasted marshmallows

Toast marshmallows on a skewer over stove burner. <u>Important</u>: be sure to hold skewer with a pot holder!

Put skewer and toasted marshmallows on a plate or aluminum foil to cool.

Break candy bars in half. You now have 4 pieces. Put a piece of candy on 4 graham crackers. Put a marshmallow on top of candy, then cover with another graham cracker. Makes 4 s'mores.

Magical No Cook Candy

You can turn this candy into many kinds, depending on what you add to the basic recipe. Then you can change it some more by molding it into different shapes.

About basic recipe:
Make it and divide it into 2 parts.
Color parts different colors with food coloring. If you like, add flavorings, (maple, lemon, vanilla, peppermint).
Add $\frac{1}{2}$ teaspoon to each part of candy.

You need:
$\frac{1}{3}$ cup butter
$\frac{1}{3}$ cup light corn syrup
1 teaspoon vanilla
$\frac{1}{2}$ teaspoon salt
1 box powdered sugar
food coloring

Magical No Cook Candy -(Continued)

Sift the powdered sugar on wax paper. Save it. Blend butter, corn syrup, vanilla, and salt in a large bowl. Add powdered sugar all at once. Mix, first with a spoon, and then with your hands. Add food coloring if you want colored candy. Keep mixing until mixture is smooth. Roll into long rolls on cutting board. Pinch off pieces and shape them the way you want them. Decorate with nuts, chocolate chips, colored sugar, or leave plain. Let harden and eat.

Marshmallow Treats

You need:
½ cube butter
About 40 regular size marshmallows
6 cups Rice Krispies or 2 packages dry Chinese noodles (the crisp kind)
¼ cup peanut butter (If you like).

Take out a baking pan with sides. Butter it well. (Rub a little butter over the bottom of the pan). Melt marshmallows on <u>low</u> heat. Melt the ½ cube of butter <u>slowly</u> in a big pot. Take pot off the stove (use pot holders) and turn off stove. Stir in melted marshmallows. (If you are going to put in peanut butter, add it now).

Add Rice Krispies or Chinese noodles to the butter. Stir well with a spoon. Press mixture into pan. Cool. Cut into squares and serve.

142

Popcorn Balls

Cook ½ cup molasses with corn syrup until thermometer reads hard crack stage - about 270°. Stir in butter and salt.

Have the popcorn in a bowl. Slowly stir in the mixture with a wooden spoon. Coat all the popcorn.

<u>Important</u>: butter your hands lightly and shape the popcorn into balls. Make them the size you want. Set them on wax paper and let them harden. Wrap the ones you don't eat with wax paper.

You need:
candy thermometer
molasses - ½ cup
corn syrup - ½ cup
butter - 1½ cubes
salt
popcorn - 8 cups

👀 Watch out for hot syrup!

143

Doggone Good Fudge

You need:
3 packages chocolate chips
1 cube butter (leave out of refrigerator)
1 pint jar marshmallow cream
2 cups nuts
1 tablespoon vanilla
1 teaspoon salt
1 tall can evaporated milk
$4\frac{1}{2}$ cups sugar

Put in a bowl: Marshmallow cream, chocolate chips, nuts, vanilla, salt and the cube of butter (cut up.) Set aside.

In a large pan mix evaporated milk and sugar. Boil 9 minutes. Take off heat. Pour over ingredients in bowl. Mix well. Pour in a cake pan. Refrigerate overnight. Hands off till tomorrow when fudge has set. Cut in cubes and eat.

144

You need:

4 packages of un-flavored gelatine

1 cup cold water

3 small packages of jello (a flavor you like)

$\frac{1}{2}$ cup sugar

4 cups boiling water

Finger Jello

Won't melt! Great to take anywhere!

You can make this in one shallow pan. A 9 x 13$\frac{1}{2}$ x 2 inch pan is a good size.

Put the ingredients in the pan in the order given, adding the boiling water last. Stir until everything is well mixed. Let set in refrigerator overnight, then cut into 1 inch cubes. Leave plain or lightly roll in powdered sugar. Take in your lunch in a plastic bag.

You need:

3 small packages of jello (different colors and flavors)
1 cup sugar ($\frac{1}{3}$ cup for each layer)
4 envelopes un-flavored gelatine ($1\frac{1}{3}$ envelopes per layer)
5 cups boiling water ($1\frac{2}{3}$ cups per layer)
$1\frac{1}{2}$ teaspoon lemon juice ($\frac{1}{2}$ teaspoon per layer)

Jello Yokan

Like Finger Jello but in 3 rainbow layers! Won't melt!

Put 1 package jello, $\frac{1}{3}$ cup sugar, and $1\frac{1}{3}$ envelopes of un-flavored gelatine in a large shallow bowl (or pan). Add $1\frac{2}{3}$ cups boiling water. Stir well. Add $\frac{1}{2}$ teaspoon lemon juice. Let set 15-20 minutes in refrigerator. Mix in a bowl: 1 package of jello (the next color and flavor), $\frac{1}{3}$ cup sugar, $1\frac{1}{3}$ envelopes of un-flavored gelatine, $1\frac{2}{3}$ cups boiling water, and $\frac{1}{2}$ teaspoon lemon juice. Stir well. Pour this over the first layer. Let set in

146

Jello Yokan* - (Continued)

refrigerator 15-20 minutes. Mix the last layer in a bowl. (1 package jello, $\frac{1}{3}$ cup sugar, $1\frac{1}{3}$ envelopes unflavored gelatine, $1\frac{2}{3}$ cups boiling water, and $\frac{1}{2}$ teaspoon lemon juice). Pour this last layer over the rest of the jello. Let it all set overnight in the refrigerator. Cut it into cubes. It's so pretty, and great to eat too!

* Yokan means
jello in Japanese.

Ice Cream Specials

Milkshake

Put ice cream in a bowl. Add milk. Mix together then beat with an egg beater. If you have adult help use a blender or electric mixer.

Pour and drink.

You need:

½ cup milk
2 scoops of
ice cream
you like

egg beater

Popsicles

You need:
Package of koolaid
Pitcher
Popsicle molds with sticks, or small plastic cups with lids.
(Have someone cut a slit in the lid. Insert stick or spoon).

Make koolaid in a pitcher, following directions on package. Pour koolaid into popsicle molds or small cups. Make sure to put in a popsicle stick. Put in freezer. Leave for about 3 hours, then eat.

Special added attractions:
Lemonade makes an extra good popsicle. Or, drop a cherry or raisins into cup with koolaid before freezing.

Floats

You need:

Cola or
7-up or
Root beer
*
Scoop of
vanilla
ice cream

Fill a glass half full with the drink you like. Add a big scoop of ice cream. Add more drink if there is room.

* Any soda drink will do. You can experiment with combinations of drink and ice cream flavors.

Chocolate Soda

You need:

2 tablespoons chocolate syrup

plain soda water

1 scoop of chocolate or vanilla ice cream

Shaker can of whipped cream.

Put the chocolate syrup in a tall glass. Add $\frac{1}{4}$ cup soda and mix. Put the scoop of ice cream in the glass carefully. Add enough soda water to fill the glass. Squirt whipped cream on top.

Ice Cream Clowns

You need:
Ice cream
Large, flat
 round cookies
gum drops or
candy hearts
shaker can of
whipped cream
ice cream
cones

Make as many as you like and freeze. This recipe is for one.

Put a scoop of ice cream in a cone. Put the cookie on the ice cream. Place the cookie and cone on the table turned over so the cone hat is up. Decorate with gum drops (candy hearts for Valentine's Day). Spray a whipped cream ruffle on the cookie. Freeze until ready to serve.

Secret to working with ice cream: Work quickly!

154

Snowballs

You need:
ice cream - your favorite
scoop
shredded coconut
maraschino cherries

Scoop a round ball of ice cream. Place on wax paper that has been spread with coconut. Roll until all covered. Place in a container and freeze. Do each one separately. Work fast. Ice cream melts! Place a cherry on top to serve. Fun for Christmas or any time!

Santa, Have a Snowball!

155

Ice Cream Cake

You need:

3 quarts of ice cream (flavors you like)
springalator pan (it opens up) ⬭
2 boxes Nabisco wafers (cookies)

Put ice cream cartons in the sink until soft. Line pan with cookies. Pour one flavor of ice cream in the pan. Top with a layer of cookies. Put in another layer of ice cream, then cookies. Put in last layer of ice cream and a topping you like. Freeze. Spring pan open and serve.

Hot Fudge Sundae

You need:
vanilla ice
cream
chocolate
or fudge
topping
can of
whipped
cream
chopped
nuts
maraschino cherry

Scoop vanilla ice cream into a dessert dish. Pour fudge topping in a pan and heat. When heated, pour over ice cream. Shake whipped cream on top. Add chopped nuts and a maraschino cherry if you like.

Lazy Daisy Banana Split
(Easy to Fix)

You need:

3 flavors of ice cream   banana chocolate and strawberry sauce

small can of crushed pineapple

* Also shaker can of whipped cream.

Peel and slice a banana. (Slice it the long way. 🍌) Put it in a dish. Scoop 3 different flavors of ice cream on top. Then pour over everything: crushed pineapple, chocolate sauce, strawberry sauce. (Any others you want would be fine). If you like, use a shaker can of whipped cream and spray the ice cream. Add a maraschino cherry.

158

Chocolate Covered Banana

You need:
chocolate candy
  bar
banana
wooden skewer
  or round pop-
  sicle stick
double boiler

Put water in the bottom part of a double boiler. Put chocolate bar in top of double boiler. Melt over medium heat. (Cooking this way, over water, keeps chocolate from burning. If you don't have a double boiler, put chocolate bar in a pan and set that pan in a frying pan with water in it.) If chocolate is too thick, add a tiny bit of milk and beat it in.

Peel banana. Stick skewer in for handle. Dip into chocolate and turn until covered. Put on waxed paper in freezer. Hardens fast.

Drinks

7-Up Fluffy Punch
for a party

You need:
punch bowl
7-Up (enough to half fill punch bowl)
½ gallon of sherbert (your favorite flavor)

Put sherbert into punch bowl. Pour in 7-Up <u>slowly</u>. It will be fizzy. Let it stay for 5 minutes. Serve. Delicious!

161

Hot Cocoa

Great with graham crackers or with a marshmallow on top.

You need:
1 tablespoon cocoa
1 tablespoon sugar
$\frac{1}{4}$ cup hot water
2 cups milk
$\frac{1}{4}$ teaspoon vanilla
marshmallows

Put cocoa and sugar into a pan. Add the hot water. Keep stirring. Bring to a boil. Boil 3 minutes.

Add a sprinkle of salt and the milk. Cook until hot but not boiling. Add the vanilla. Pour into cups. Put a marshmallow on top.

Variation: Sprinkle with cinnamon for a different taste!

162

Lemonade
Makes 6 Glasses

You need:
⅓ cup lemon juice
¼ cup sugar
1 quart cold water
ice cubes

If you use fresh lemons, cut in half and squeeze enough lemon juice to make ⅓ of a cup. Put into a tall pitcher. Add 1 cup of water and the sugar. Stir until the sugar is dissolved. Add the rest of the water and stir. Taste. If you want it sweeter add a little more sugar. Add ice cubes and it is ready to drink.

Bug Juice Punch

Any kind of punch mix will do. Add one or more kinds of things you like:

raisins	dried apricots - cut up
apple bits	strawberries
banana slices	cherries

We like apple cider and raisins. See what you can invent.

Bug Juice
5¢

Strawberry Flip

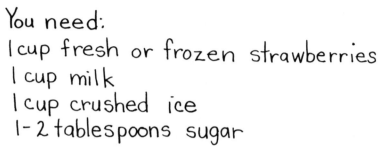

You need:
1 cup fresh or frozen strawberries
1 cup milk
1 cup crushed ice
1-2 tablespoons sugar

Clean and cut up strawberries. Crush ice with an ice crusher (or wrap ice in a dish towel, place on a cutting board, and hit it with a hammer). Mix all ingredients for 1 minute in a blender, or shake well in a covered plastic container. Makes 2 servings.

Shimmy Shakes

Pour 2 cups of juice into plastic container. Add milk or milk powder, vanilla, and crushed ice. Shake until smooth.

You need:

1 quart plastic container + lid

2 cups cold juice (your favorite)

½ cup powdered milk or 1 cup fresh milk

½ teaspoon vanilla

crushed ice*

Special Added attraction:

One scoop of ice cream makes an extra good shake.

*If you don't have crushed ice, put 3 cubes of ice in a towel. Put on cutting board and hit ice with a hammer.

Eggnog

You need:

rotary egg beater
or blender
4 eggs OOOO
½ cup sugar
¼ teaspoon salt
4 cups cold milk
1 teaspoon vanilla
nutmeg

First beat the eggs with the sugar and salt. Slowly pour in the milk. Add the vanilla. Keep beating until well mixed.

Pour into glasses and drink. Add ice and a sprinkle of nutmeg if you like.

<u>Special added attraction</u>: Keep eggnog in refrigerator. Just before bedtime <u>slowly</u> heat 1 cup. Drink and sweet dreams.

Russian Easter Eggs

You need:
Eggs - uncooked
Pin
Bowl
Any of these:
marking pens
water colors
crayons
colored paper
and paste

Remove eggs from the refrigerator. Let stand about ½ hour. Hold egg over bowl. Poke holes in both ends of the eggshell with pin. Blow egg out of shell into bowl by blowing in one hole. Rinse eggs gently in water and dry. Decorate however you like. You can tope a thread to each egg and hang from a dried branch Egg-tree.

Piñata Party

You need:
- Large shopping bag
- Wrapped candy
- Newspaper
- Tissue paper— many colors
- Scissors
- Glue
- Stick, bat or broom.

Get a large shopping bag. Fill it lightly with crinkled newspaper. Put wrapped candy inside too. Close the bag. Now decorate!

Cut tissue paper into 3 inch strips. Cut fringe in each strip. Glue the strips around the bag. Start at the bottom or at one side. Overlap. Add legs, ears, face, or any idea you have.

Hang the piñata for a party. One player at a time tries to break the piñata — blindfolded. He will be using a stick to try to break it so, <u>stand back</u>. Watch the candy

Piñata - (Continued)

when it is broken. Fun
and candy for
everyone!

Variation: You can
also stuff the piñata
with small party favors,
or small bags of
treats with individual
names on them.
     Great fun!

Shooting Stars - (Continued)

You need:
Popcorn
Butter
Salt
Electric
popcorn
popper
Clean but
old sheet
Big brown
bag

Spread out clean sheet on floor. Put popcorn popper in the middle. Plug it in.

Let your friends sit in a circle around the popper. (Not too close!) Put popcorn in popper and leave off the lid. Sit and watch the popcorn fireworks.

After the shower of fireworks (popcorn) put popcorn in a bag. Add butter and salt. Shake and serve. Remember to unplug popper!

Sugar Eggs

Very easy to make but egg mold is needed.

You need:

2 cups superfine
  sugar (1 box)
3 teaspoons water
food coloring
egg mold - They
come in many
sizes in plastic
and metal. Can
be found in dime
stores and cooking
specialty shops.

Sugar Eggs - (Continued)

Mix the sugar and water in a bowl. (You can mix it with your hands). Add a <u>little</u> food coloring if you want a colored egg. Mix until it is like wet sand — no lumps.

Pack the mixture in the mold (both halves) ⌣ ⌣. Fill to the top. Turn out on a cutting board to dry.

After 2 hours, scoop out the centers with a spoon. Cut the tip off with a string.

Put Easter grass, little pictures, jelly beans, whatever you like, on the bottom of one half. Use white glue to hold the top on. Frost the front with icing (any color you like). Icing recipe is on following page. front of egg
frosting

Sugar Egg Frosting

You need:

An egg separator	food coloring
1 cup powdered sugar	icing bag
$\frac{1}{4}$ teaspoon cream of tartar	1 egg white
$\frac{1}{3}$ cup boiling water	beater or mixer

Put the egg separator over a cup. Break the egg in. The egg white will be separated from the yolk. Put the egg white and other ingredients in the bowl. (<u>Not</u> the yolk!) Add a few drops of food coloring (1 color). Beat until frosting stands in peeks. This takes about 8 minutes. Put into icing bag and frost the edge of the sugar egg. Let it set, then peek in.

Index

Dinners

Vegetables

Sandwiches

180

Nitty Gritty Productions appreciates the artistic efforts of the following young artists whose drawings appear in this book:

Maria Ala p. 88
Ana Maria Barajas p. 153
Jill Balthazar p. 28
Michelle Bissell pp. 57, 168
Marie Collins - Last Page in Book
Theresa Flores p. 80
Soccoro Jaregui p. 36
Maria Jiminez p. 93
Robbie Johnston p. 136
Shelley Kim p. 9
Stacey Lee - First Page in Book

Raymone G. Mijares p. 108
Elvira Mora - Next to Title Page
Benton Poole p. 121
Eva Portillo pp. 48, 128
Miguel Reyes p. 65
Philip Rossovich p. 116
Lori Rovetta pp. 100, 148
Lori Saraceni p. 72
Cheryl Shelmadine p. 16
Theresa Valadez pp. 44, 160
Orlando Vasquez - Next to
Introduction

Metric Conversion Chart

Liquid or Dry Measuring Cup (Based on 8 oz. cup)

$\frac{1}{4}$ cup = 60 ml
$\frac{1}{3}$ cup = 80 ml
$\frac{1}{2}$ cup = 125 ml
$\frac{3}{4}$ cup = 190 ml
1 cup = 250 ml
2 cups = 500 ml

Liquid or Dry Teaspoon and Tablespoon

$\frac{1}{4}$ teaspoon = 1.5 ml
$\frac{1}{2}$ teaspoon = 3 ml
1 teaspoon = 5 ml
3 teaspoons = 1 tablespoon or 15 ml

Pan Sizes (1 inch = 25 mm)

8-inch pan, round or square = 200 mm x 200 mm
9-inch pan, round or square = 225 x 225 mm
9 x 5 x 3-inch loaf pan = 225 mm x 125 mm x 75 mm
$\frac{1}{4}$ inch thickness = 5 mm
$\frac{1}{8}$ inch thickness = 2.5 mm

Mass

1 ounce = 30 g
4 ounces = $\frac{1}{4}$ pound = 125 g
8 ounces = $\frac{1}{2}$ pound = 250 g
16 ounces = 1 pound = 500 g
2 pounds = 1 k

Temperatures

°F		°C
200	=	100
250	=	120
275	=	140
300	=	150
325	=	160
350	=	180
375	=	190
400	=	200
425	=	220
450	=	230

Key

ml = milliliter
l = liter
g = gram
oz. = ounce